PACKING LIGHT,
PACKING RIGHT!

**The Sound *RIDER!* guide to
motorcycle packing**

By Tom Mehren

Mixed Media
2226 Eastlake Ave E #69
Seattle, WA 98102
www.mm411.com

Also available from Mixed Media

Motorcycle Restoration 101, Tom Mehren

Motorcycle 101, Dave Preston

The SR! Guide to Riding the Columbia River Gorge, Tom Mehren

The Essential Guide to Owning, Riding and Maintaining Dirt Bikes, Tory Briggs

MIXED MEDIA PRODUCTION TEAM

Publisher
Tom Mehren

Editing
Patrick Duff
Connie Adams

Layout, Design & Image Making
Tom Mehren
Patrick Duff

Printing
Gorham Printing, WA

Back Office & Antics
Fox Muldar
Dana Scully

Special thanks: Patrick Duff and Connie Adams for their work on this book. David Hough for his added wisdom and input. All the dealers and manufacturers who put up with me year after year, and the readers of Sound RIDER! who inspired me to write this book.

Dear Mom,

I suppose we both could have figured out that this was going to happen. You remember that time when I was 10 and all the other kids were getting bikes and I told you I needed one – not 'wanted' one Mom, I 'needed' one.

But you told me not over your dead body until I was 18. You were, however, wise enough to allow me to own my own helmet and gloves and you knew every time I rode away on my bicycle 'geared up' where I was going.

And so the desire grew over eight years and not a day after I turned 18 low and behold there was a motorcycle in our driveway. It was nice of Billy Holbrook to decide not to take motorcycling up after all, putting only 600 miles on that XL100 before he sold it to me for $600.

And today Mom, well you know what's going on cause we talk about it every week. I've got five bikes in the garage, I publish a motorcycle magazine and this is my third book about riding motorcycles.

I shudder to think, Mom, where my life would have gone had you let me get a bike when I was 'ready' for one at ten! We can both see that making me wait was good medicine ingraining that desire to own my own bike into my cortex for so many years.

So Mom, this book is dedicated to you for having the foresight that you did.

Table of Contents

Please note: Items marked with **SR!** in this book can be purchased online through the Sound RIDER! store at:

www.soundrider.com/store

For book updates, to see other people's lists, read tales from the road, share your comments and links to more resources visit:

www.soundrider.com/plpr

Introduction

This book is meant to be a useful guide to motorcycle touring. It's filled with information about what to pack, what to leave home and how to do it intelligently. It won't tell you where to go, but how to get there as simply as possible so you can have an enjoyable trip without burdening yourself with too much gear and missing out on items that will ease your travel.

With just three pieces of hard luggage this rider has all the space he needs to travel for multiple days.

Several years ago I began creating lists of what to bring on my rides. This of course occurred from countless times of winding up somewhere without the right gear. Whether it was a day ride or an overnight trip, before I was making lists I always wound up without an important staple in my motorcycling diet. One ride I would carry something, another I wouldn't - and that would be the ride when I needed it.

After getting into the list-making aspect I began having a much better time on rides. If you get allergies, you know that riding is no fun if your eyes are watering or you're sneezing. This was just one aspect that improved after creating lists, so I remembered to pack the allergy medicine every time.

As a magazine publisher in the Northwest, I began lecturing on what to pack and what not to pack. It started as a favor to a motorcycle accessories store, escalated to a lecture hall full of our readers and eventually it became apparent someone needed to write a book about this. Why not me? I took up the task with pleasure as I've always enjoyed writing books to help others based on my own experiences.

As a kid I used to go backpacking for several days at a stretch. Eventually, I gave it up after dealing with several physical ailments including chronic sciatica and a bum left knee. I thought I would never camp out again. Fine with me; back then sleeping on the ground in the cold was never too fun anyway.

Ten years later I began producing motorcycle rallies and touring on two wheels extensively. I sucked it up and bought a new tent and sleeping bag. Technology has come a long way since my old backpacking days and instead of having a lousy time as expected, I truly enjoyed camping while motorcycle touring. In fact, today it's my preferred mode of touring.

One drawback for all of us has been the weight of the gear we need to carry. So I drilled down deeper, found lighter and smaller items and today I actually find I have extra space in my gear bags. Now imagine that.

I also put on a number of events each year that involve 150 to 300 mile days for riders. For those people this book may offer some insight to enjoying their time more in the saddle during those long hours, as well as when they bed down at night. The book wasn't meant as a handbook for Iron Butt riders who run 1,000 miles in 18 hours – there are other books for that. It's also not going to give you all the tips you need if you travel outside the United States. I think Greg Frazier did a pretty good job of that with his books, Riding the World (Bow Tie Press 2005), and Motorcycle Touring (Motorbooks 2005).

This book is not a riding skills book. David Hough does a fine job of authoring books on riding skills through his Street Strategies and Proficient Motorcycle series published through Bow Tie and available in the Sound RIDER! online store.

Will you save money with this book? Probably. Once you've dialed in your touring gear to where it should be, you'll find yourself spending less money on needless items that really don't belong on your ride. How many things do you currently own that don't go on the road with you anymore? Is it time for a garage sale perhaps?

Shameless plugs? I'll cover a lot of items in this book. Some you can buy at motorcycle shops, others at outdoor gear stores. Items that we sell in the Sound *RIDER!* store are marked with an **SR!** so that you know you can pick them up online there. The Sound *RIDER!* store was created as a convenience store for the motorcycle touring enthusiast. Consider it a one-stop-shop for the hard-to-find gear you'll need when you travel.

This book is a culmination of wisdom learned by visiting many motorcycle and outdoor gear stores, riding thousands of miles and spending many happy nights in motels, hotels and on the ground. I wish you the best on your next trip wherever you go. Riding motorcycles is a lot of fun. Touring on them smartly is a blast. See you on the road!

Loaded down! – This bike is carrying three pieces of hard luggage, five exterior bags stuffed to the gills and a rider of course. We can all travel lighter than this. Can you imagine how it might be maneuvering this beast in a 40 mph windstorm?

Chapter One

The Basics

Traveling Light

It's the 21st century. A lot of technology occurred in the last two decades that made it possible for outdoor enthusiasts to drop cargo weight. Riding gear is lighter, clothing is lighter, luggage is lighter and camping gear is lighter.

And lighter is better when we talk about riding our motorcycles. A lighter bike is more agile when it comes to handling, winding your way through a series of sweeper curves, maneuvering an obstacle and finding a parking spot. But how about picking up your bike when it falls over – with all your gear packed on for a multi-day ride. The less it all weighs, the better your ride will be.

Packing Smaller

How much space will you need on your bike to pack for a five-day-motorcycle trip? At some point you may have packed for a trip like this, and when you stepped back and looked at your bike it had turned into something resembling a wooly 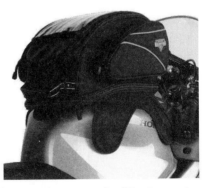 mammoth (like the one on the previous page). You're not alone. When you're selecting the essentials you need to

carry consider everythings size. It all adds up in the end and if you select a few oversize versions of items you need, all of a sudden you find you're out of space.

A tailpack, like this one from PacSafe and a tank bag like the Nelson-Rigg model shown on the previous page provide enough storage to carry all you need for a simple day ride.

Staying Dryer – Dump Your Cotton!

When it comes to clothing, the rule of thumb is – dump your cotton. Cotton is evil for motorcyclists because it absorbs and retains water, weighs a ton compared to synthetics, uses more space and takes forever to dry out. This includes cotton blue jeans, sweat shirts, cotton t-shirts, underwear, socks and hats. Leave them at home.

When you're selecting items for your trip keep in mind the fascinating advances in the technology of synthetics over the last two decades. They wick water away from the body, dry about six times faster and weigh far less than their cotton counterparts and pack up much smaller. A sweaty pair of socks can cause you to get hypothermia when you hit the mountain pass, your sweatshirt is eating up precious space in your luggage, and waiting around for cotton to come out of the dryer at the Timbuktu Laundromat is eating away at your travel time.

Is it Multipurpose?

One way to cut
down how much
you carry is to
evaluate how
many uses an item
has. Consider
how much space a
separate knife,
wire cutters, nail

clippers and a corkscrew take up. A multipurpose tool,
such as a Leatherman tool, which includes all these devices
and a half dozen more will cut that space by 75%. That's a
great savings in both weight and size. As you select your
items for touring look for those that are multipurpose –
there are many.

*The Leatherman Tool shown above has more than a dozen
uses and packs up about the size of two pocket knives
making it a compact companion to have on the road.*

Minimize Your Fatigue

That guy in the SUV on the cell phone driving forty in a
fifty is definitely causing you fatigue, but there are a
number of other things during your ride that cause fatigue
and you may not even be aware of them. Sweaty
underwear is causing you to switch back and forth on your
seat, your socks sliding below your ankles is creating the
desire to pull them up – but you can't at sixty miles an
hour; your overheated body has you looking for a drink of
water every time you take a turn and so on. And these are
just some of the things stealing your awareness of what is
going on around you and enjoying the scenery you're

passing through. This book has a lot of suggestions for you about things that may lessen your fatigue and allow you to ride more competently for longer periods of time.

Buy Quality

As we discuss various items throughout the book, keep in mind quality. Motorcycling is inherently tough on anything associated with it. Whether it's gear, prescriptions or your body, everything on a motorcycle ride is bouncing around mile after mile.

This can wreak havoc on products that are not built well. Sure you can get a $19 air pump at the auto parts store but it won't last as long as a durable pump that costs $100. And when you need it most, that's when it will fail.

Cheap tents that cost $49 are no fun when they start leaking, more often than not all too early in their life. You'll have to pay more to get a better quality shelter but the expense is worth it in terms of a more enjoyable trip and the piece of mind that comes with it.

Same goes for riding gear. Buy the good stuff and it will last you much longer making it more of a value over time.

Chapter Two

Riding Gear Selection

We begin with selecting our riding gear. What you put on in the morning is as important as what you carry in your bags. I couldn't write this book about motorcycle touring without covering these everyday essentials.

Geared Up – While jeans and open-face helmets may be a popular way to dress, this rider isn't taking any chances when it comes to road rash by wearing a full-face helmet with armored textile gear and leather motorcycle boots.

Helmet

I own property in Hawaii, where to date there is no helmet law, and I'm still amazed at how many people ride in that state without a helmet and opt to put their family in the position of deciding whether they continue life support or not. As a motorcycle magazine publisher I get letters all the time about a loved one who crashed and died. Inevitably they were wearing a ¾, ½ shell, or no shell at all.

We all know that helmets aren't the end-all to surviving a crash, but the evidence is obvious that an approved helmet provides the best chances for the least amount of injury and care after. There are those who fight for freedom when it comes to helmet laws. The smart freedom is knowing that nowhere in the world is a helmet considered illegal.

There's an old adage when you're shopping for a helmet. 'What's your head worth? Do you have a $100 head or a $500 head?'

Helmets are designed to keep your brain from bruising itself against the cranium in the event of a crash. This does not mean they will keep your head from splitting, but they will lessen the impact greatly. At least a full-face helmet will, perhaps a ¾ helmet will but who wants to land face down in a ¾ helmet? Let's not even conjure up the image of what you'd look like when you hit the pavement in a ½ shell helmet.

Okay, so you get the drift that I'm a proponent of the full-face over a ¾ or ½ shell helmet. Right. I've been brainwashed into thinking a full-face helmet will offer me the best protection in the event of a crash. I haven't found anything to the contrary to date so I'm sticking with the facts already on record at the Head Protection Research Laboratory.

I once toured with a man who lived in a state without a helmet law. He didn't wear one. He came to my state and had to wear one. He chose a full-face. It takes about 500 miles to get used to the darn things before you figure out it's not such a big deal to wear one. Wear one long enough and you'll feel naked with anything less.

Jacket

What type of jacket you wear will depend on the season. If you like to ride in the winter, chances are you won't wear the same jacket during the summer.

In the summer I typically wear mesh gear; in the fall, winter and spring I have an entirely different jacket I wear. But the two jackets share several common features. They both have body armor at the hit points which are the elbows and shoulders, they both have reflective surfaces on them and they both would hold together for a slide that begins at 60 mph for at least twenty feet.

There are a number of jackets sold on the market today that look great but don't have protective padding and wouldn't last 10 feet in a slide. What's more important – look fashionable, or not break an arm? Protective padding can mean the difference of having a fractured or broken bone, or simply a bruise. I'll take the bruise, thank you. When you shop for a jacket, look for these attributes and don't be afraid to ask the sales person for statistics on what they sell. A few will actually know. You can also learn more by visiting a manufacturer's website.

Jacket liners are good too. Regardless of the season it's nice to have a liner with some warmth and a wind stopper coating to keep you warmer on chilly mornings. You can even get this as part of a mesh jacket setup.

If you plan to ride into cold conditions below about 40 degrees, consider an electric vest or liner.

Pants

There are those who think a pair of denim jeans is all they need when they ride. There are three important points to remember here (and you might be able to come up with a few more of your own). Denim jeans typically grind through the flesh after sliding on pavement for about four feet. And if you've never gotten the chance to crash test them by now, surely you must know that riding in a hot sweaty pair of denim jeans is about as fun as sucking lima beans through a straw. And when your jeans get wet on Wednesday, they might be dry by Friday.

Just like jackets, look for durable gear that has armor at all the hit points. For summer get a mesh pair, for the other seasons get a solid leather or textile set and be sure they each have a liner that can be zipped in and out.

How about chaps? Here's the deal on chaps. Back in the old days, and we're talking the cattle ranching days of the 1800s, someone came up with leather chaps as a way to reduce abrasion from tumble weeds, brambles and brush, and to keep horse sweat off the rider. They worked well for that and still do today. But wear them on a motorcycle? Why? You still get wet in the crotch when it rains, they provide no protection to your butt when you go into a slide, they have no padding at the hit points, they weigh a ton and eat up a lot of space in your luggage.

Below is a grid that shows how many feet a rider will slide on pavement before the material around them disintegrates.

Denim Jeans	Armored Kevlar Textile Motorcycle Gear	Armored Competition Weight Leather Motorcycle Gear
4 feet	20 feet	80+ feet

These numbers are based on a 175 pound rider and good quality gear. Your results may vary. Bottom line – get out of the blue jeans and into something more protective.

If you wear armored textile riding pants, do you need to wear some kind of street pants underneath? Nope. If it's 85 degrees outside and you plan to don protective textile over-pants, you don't need to put pants on underneath, simply slip them over your naked legs and ride.

Many companies make armored mesh pants which will keep you cooler on a warm day than any cotton pant will.

Boots

This is another area where fashion dukes it out with practicality. I've seen all kinds of boots come to the market. Some make a lot of sense, others you could play basketball in.

I see a lot of sport riders in tennis shoes or sandals during the summer months. I hope you weren't thinking of wearing tennis shoes on your next five day trip around the world, or down to the corner market for that matter. Feet are complex, and it's awfully painful to get them put back together again.

When shopping for a boot, if it looks agile enough to shoot hoops with, pass on it for a motorcycle boot.

Boot of choice –
The Oxtar Matrix with Gor-Tex has served me well for 100,000 miles of riding.

With motorcycle boots there are three important things to consider. First – is it waterproof, second – does it provide stiff coverage over the ankle, and third – is it light weight. Several companies produce boots that meet these criteria including Oxtar, Alpinestars and Sidi.

I once used a pair of Oxtar boots 100,000 miles after which I sent them back to the manufacturer advising them that I had enjoyed the boots for many miles, but after a 500 mile dualsport ride through Oregon I had trashed them. They promptly sent me another pair and retired the original set to their archive. Look for a boot you can get 100,000 miles out of.

Gloves

But there's a variety of gloves on the market. Some good, some better, and some that should never be worn. Look for gloves designed for motorcycle riding. Fleece mittens, leather garden gloves and the like were never designed for impact into pavement at high speed. For that you'll want to be wearing a glove with strong seams and quality leather and/or textile.

Gloves are a ritical part of our riding regalia. They protect your hands from windburn and sunburn, keep them warm in the cold, and if you take a tumble, full-fingered leather means you won't have to be picking asphalt out of your palms.And when we stop we get a chance to admire all the bugs that didn't get the chance to die crashing directly into our knuckles.

I typically take three pair of gloves on a ride with me, even if I'm just on a day ride. I carry a winter set, a medium season (spring and fall) pair and a summer set during the spring, summer and fall. Inevitably I end up wearing them all at some point on the trip. Both my winter and medium season gloves are lined with a waterproof lining that truly works – Gortex. I've seen a lot of less expensive gloves go over the counter and I've provided heat packs to a lot of those buyers to warm their hands when they inevitably get wet inside. Spend the money and get a real waterproof lining in your glove. If your winter gloves leak now, get a pair that won't.

My winter gloves are BMW and keep my hands warm all day down to about 40 degrees. If you're riding in temperatures below that for any length of time you'll need to think about getting some electric gloves, like those produced by Gerbing's Heated Clothing.

Gloves and Gauntlets *– These BMW Pro Winter gloves work nicely down to the low 40s. If it's raining, try and keep your raingear sleeve over the top of the gauntlet.*

My medium season gloves made by Held are lighter, but still offer some warmth and are fully waterproof.

Here's the deal on gloves. In all winter and medium season gloves, your hands may perspire. If they do that means there's water surrounding your hands. Even if your gloves are waterproof, they may still get wet inside – because you sweat in them. Wet hands can lead to hypothermia.

Now how do you sweat in them when it's cold outside? Well, let's suppose it's time to head up into a mountain pass, but before you do you pull out to gas up, secure your gear and have a snack at the mini mart. You're wearing cold weather gear, you dismount, gas up, walk into the mini mart to pay for the gas, grab a snack, eat it, walk around, shoot the breeze, hit the restroom, check your gear, and put your helmet back on. By now, with that cold weather gear on, you've worked up a sweat. You might not even feel it yet, but your body is emitting moisture to keep itself cool. You head 25 miles into the mountain pass and low and behold you're cold and clammy. Now you feel the moisture in your gloves. Brrrrr.

So if you plan on riding in really cold weather, consider a pair of electric gloves as your winter glove choice on the ride. Even if it's October or May, you might save yourself from an unpleasant experience.

Underwear SR!

…or shall we say underpants. Consider this the first of two times in the book when we're going to talk about our butts. In this section we're going to discuss how to keep the butt dry. Typical cotton underwear is the preferred choice by many, but not a good one when riding a motorcycle. Some wear polyester underwear in their everyday life, but few wear a polyester fabric with a wickable tricot pad, which actually makes no sense at all in everyday life, but a lot of sense when you're on two wheels.

Today when I ride I wear a polyester skin with a tricot pad made by Andiamo. The skin, being modern-day polyester and all, wicks the moisture my body perspires away from me as I ride. It also has a tricot liner that cushions me and absorbs moisture away from my body. No more sticky underwear that gets me shifting on the seat left and right in an unending battle to relieve the sticky sensations cotton underwear creates, especially on days when the temperature goes above eighty degrees. Switching around on your seat is irritating and causes fatigue and the dreaded 'Monkey-Butt'. Spend 300 miles in a day doing that, and you'll be pretty beat by sundown.

These Andiamo! skins were originally designed for casual bicyclists who wanted to turn any pair of shorts into bicycling shorts. Little did they know the skins held a lot of value for a motorcyclist. I've seen some motorcyclists, primarily dualsport riders, wear full-on cycling shorts with a gel pad and all. Interesting idea, but these are not good for the rider as the seat on our bike is too wide to allow breathability and that gel pad does nothing to absorb body moisture in the meantime.

Andiamo makes both boxer and brief styles of their products for both men and women.

Base Layers SR!

Base layers are the first layers of clothing you wear on your skin, such as a t-shirt or what some call long underwear. In the winter they may help you retain body heat, in the summer they may help you expel it. The technologies of polyesters and nylons over the last two decades have greatly improved what's available to the market for the right job.

Base layer is a fairly new term. It was first grasped by the ski industry when skiers needed a way to maintain body heat while riding up a lift. It later allowed back packers to do the same when they stopped moving and today the term is common throughout the outdoor industry. The common premise of the base layer is that no matter what, it will wick water away from your skin.

Most base layer clothing companies create their products for "Active Sports" – skiing, hiking, football, basketball and the like. For motorcyclists, we need a slightly different base layer. When we ride our motorcycles on pavement this is referred to as a "Leisure Sport" by manufacturers of base layer clothing. So the garments that are created for the active sports industry by companies like Under Armor don't always work the same way for the leisure sports people like us.

Because of this end, I worked together with Andiamo! to create a series of base layer garments specifically for motorcyclists that will help you maintain body heat during cold times and release body heat when it's hot – all while sitting on your motorcycle (doing nothing – right?). While some gear will keep you warm at 60 mph for 30 minutes, ours is designed to maintain your body heat for up to 60 minutes, but should you go indoors, as soon as the garment is met with outdoor air (you take off your jacket) then it immediately radiates heat away from your body, keeping you from overheating at room temperature.

Polyester is a really cool thing – almost literally. As soon as the air hits it directly it wicks off heat and moisture in an almost space age kind of way. There's also a shirt that will do this for you when you ride in hot air conditions. Mix a shirt like this together with an evaporative cooling vest (more about this later) and you're in for a comfortable ride – even in the desert.

Old school cotton long johns to combat the cold are a scary thought when it comes to motorcycling. At the other end of the spectrum, wearing a tank top on a hot day can cause heat stroke. Why not put on the latest technology when you ride?

Socks *SR!*

There's more technology going on here. Coolmax is a synthetic fabric that wicks away both moisture and heat during hot times and just moisture when it gets colder. It's the most flexible fabric for the motorcyclist, because it keeps the feet as dry as possible and allows warmth when needed.

Let's go back to that scenario where we're walking around the gas station just before heading into the mountain pass. Our feet are sweating too. But if we've got a pair of Coolmax socks on, the moisture from our body is being wicked away by the fabric, and it's likely our feet won't get cold before our hands.

Our feet and hands are the first things to get cold when we enter into cold conditions. It's not just a matter of discomfort and pain; freezing fingers and toes distracts us from the road ahead, slows down our reactions, and puts us in a vulnerable situation.

When buying socks consider "over the calf" length. Short socks tend to slide down and irritate the heck out of you. A lot of riders enjoy the benefits of over-the-calf socks which stay up as you ride and also keep your boot tops from chafing your shins.

If you're going to ride in very cold conditions, consider electrically-heated socks. If you plan to ride all day at 38 degrees, add a pair of electric socks to your heated clothing shopping cart.

Eyewear SR!

Seems like everywhere you go there's eyewear available in the form of some kind of sun glasses from somebody. But, when it comes to riding a motorcycle, you need eyewear that is appropriate for any riding situation. And there's good news for prescription wearers too.

Flexibility? Consider this. You wake up in the morning and it's foggy, by 10 a.m. it's partly cloudy and by 3 p.m. you're riding through the desert in full sun. Some people need to wear prescriptions. No one set of glasses can deal with all that - or is there such a thing?

For the last two years I've been wearing touring eyewear made by Global Vision, a Midwest company that sells all kinds of eyewear. Their touring eyewear has interchangeable lenses so I can switch from yellow lenses on a foggy morning, to driver lenses on a partly cloudy day, then to smoke lenses during a full-sun afternoon. The folks at Global Vision have also come up with prescription options that allow an RX frame to be inserted behind their GV Adaptables frame. They also have bi-focal reading lenses available for their C-2000 touring in clear and smoke so you can view your instruments, maps and GPS while you ride.

The important thing to remember when you tour is to take inexpensive glasses with you, but treat them like they cost hundreds of dollars. It's easy enough to pack too tight and wind up with a broken frame. That would happen as easily with an inexpensive set as it would with an expensive set of Oakley's.

Earplugs

Wind buffeting is one of the biggest evils when it comes to hearing loss (loud pipes come in second). Also called the *slow killer*, wind noise can cause hearing impairment without you even knowing it. Take it from someone who is half deaf, the last thing I want to do is lose the other half. We should also note here that exposure to noise causes both mental irritation and slowed responses, neither of which is good for the motorcyclist.

Foam earplugs provide about as much noise cancellation as rolling the windows all the way up on a Lexus. They won't entirely block out all the sound, but they will protect your hearing, reduce frustration and maintain your response times.

Look for foam earplugs that cut at least 30db off the surrounding noise levels. And don't you worry, you'll still hear sirens and alarms and people skidding along behind you.

I recently read in a motorcycle catalog where they warned about wearing foam earplugs when you ride, instead encouraging readers to wear 12db reduction earphones so they could listen to their MP3 player as they rode. My opinion: Hogwash.

Neck/Head Warmer

Thin tubes of polyester have been known to keep riders warm and even provide some protection to hair-dos during the long ride. You might want to consider packing one for the ride. The best ones offer about ten combinations of ways they can be twisted over your head from a simple neck warmer, to a full on balaclava. They weigh very little and take up almost no space at all. You can even slip them into the pocket of your coat.

Handkerchief

So I told you to dump your cotton. But if you're like me you need to clear your passages now and then so go ahead and splurge. Pack a cotton handkerchief and feel more natural and better about the day. Use it for your nose, not your glasses. More on this later in the book.

Chapter Three

Storage

There's a lot of luggage on the market: textile tank bags, metal boxes, leather bags, various panniers and on and on. How you organize your gear when it's in your luggage is another consideration. Let's sort this all out.

Tank Bag *SR!*

If you have the ability to travel with a tank bag on your bike, take advantage. It's a convenient place to store items you'll need throughout the day like credit cards, cell phone, camera, eyewear cleaner, your hat and so on. They come in a lot of sizes. I tend to prefer medium size bags that come with a waterproof cover such as those designed by Nelson-Rigg. The smaller ones don't have the capacity I need and the oversize ones tend to block the view of my instruments. I'll take a magnetic bag over a strap on any day, because I can get it on and off with the most ease. But some don't have the option since a number of bikes on the market today are plastic coated over the assumed tank area.

Tail Pack *SR!*

When I go out for an all day ride, I use my tail pack to store items such as water, rain gear, a fleece vest and spare gloves. Again there's a lot on the market and again I go for the medium size versions. The tail pack I currently sport is made by PacSafe and features mesh webbing between the fabric and a cable lock. I can lock it down and keep the honest people honest when I'm away from the bike.

I didn't always carry a tail pack. And when I didn't, I never had enough room for everything I needed to have on the road. Once I started riding with the combination of a tank bag and tail pack I actually had more room then I needed -- which was great.

I use a larger tail pack when I tour overnight. It's made by Nelson-Rigg and snaps together to my soft saddle bags so all three become a single unit. It features expandable pockets and comes with a rain cover. There are also several tie down points on it so I can thread cargo straps through them and tie down larger items over the top.

Saddle Bags

These come in all sizes and materials. You need to decide what's right for you. Many cruiser and sport touring bikes already have saddle bags installed either as hard cases or leather units. For the rest of us we have to decide which way to go.

Large metal panniers (side boxes) are available from companies like Happy Trails, Jesse and Touratech. They're not cheap, but they keep out dust, water and sticky fingers. The drawbacks are that they can become severely damaged in a crash, or even cause a crash as we saw with one rider who passed what he thought was a bush only to find out there was a large rock behind it. The severity of the impact sheared the bag right off his bike. After lots of zip ties and duct tape, the rider limped into the next town and found a blacksmith to aid with a better repair.

I prefer soft bags, which are fairly flexible during a crash, are easy to get on and off the bike and weigh considerably less. The drawbacks are they can be a thieves paradise if you leave them alone on the bike, if not properly fitted they can sag into the suspension or melt on a hot muffler and they notoriously leak in heavy rainfall. Nelson-Rigg solved the leaky bag issue by providing a set of dry bags with some of their saddle bags. That way the items inside stay dry and can be easily removed at the end the day.

Leather saddle bags may or may not leak, depending on the quality and how much water is hitting them. Leather, no matter what, will absorb water. How hard it's raining will determine how soon and how much. Rain can double the weight of the leather and eventually wet leather will lose it's shape.

Mesh Totes, Compression Sacks & Dry Bags *SR!*

What's the best way to store your items in the tank bag, tail pack and saddle bags? I've found see-through mesh totes to offer the best solution. I organize like things together into single bags. For instance, I store my medicines, wind and sun protection, etc. all in one place, and I can actually see where they are in the mesh tote so I can access them quickly.

Mesh totes come in lots of sizes, and I also use them to store my spare gloves, clothing and rain gear. They come in handy if you wind up with wet camp shoes or want to sort your clean laundry from the dirty stuff.

One reader suggested having different colored totes to help identify what is inside. Makes good sense. Another attribute I like about them is they weigh next to nothing.

I store overnight clothing and my sleeping bag in dry bags. For my tent and other bulky items I want to make small, I use a compression sack or two.

From spring to fall I carry an evaporative cooling vest. I store it in a #1 size dry bag. When it's time to hydrate it, I simply fill the bag with water with the garment inside, wait ten minutes and I'm ready to be cooled down.

When loading your storage sacks, place them vertically into your luggage instead of one atop the other. This makes for easier access to everything at any time.

Nite Ize Multi Pock-Its Holsters SR!

My tank bag tends to get a little cluttered, so I've come up with a modular system using a series of Nite Ize Multi Pock-Its holsters.

These were originally designed to be used one at a time on a belt to hold various gadgetry such as cell phones, pen lights, pens, credit cards, PDAs and so on. I've found I can connect three together, place them into my tank bag and have easy access to my camera, GPS, cell phone, Leatherman tool, Mag Lite, pens, and a lot of other items that used to roll around loosely or had to be packed into their own individual carrying case.

A combination of 3 Nite Ize holsters holding a camera, GPS, cell phone, flashlight, eyewear, pens, Leatherman and much more.

Freezer Bags

Freezer bags are good at keeping things dry and keeping dirty items separate from the clean ones. For example I store my matches in a freezer bag, my chain oil and rag in another, and my eyewear cleaning solution and cloth in another.

Get good quality freezer bags that seal like those made by Ziploc. Avoid thinner sandwich bags. You don't want to have a thin plastic bag become torn during your next road trip and find liquids leaking in your luggage.

Cargo Straps *SR!*

It's good to carry a pair or two of top quality cargo straps to tie down large items. I've seen variations of bungees, but the ones I like best are made by RokStraps. There are no metal parts on a RokStrap, you simply loop each end over a grab bar, or tie down loop, then snap it together. The fifty four inch versions are adjustable down to eighteen inches making them useful for all kinds of applications, whether you need to tie down a jacket or a combination of tent, sleeping bag and air mattress.

Another item I like to carry is a six-point cargo net with six nylon hook points on it. This I've found convenient for tying down my atlas case or securing small cargo on a trip around town.

Locks and Security
SR!

PacSafe has a number of security devices I like to use when I travel. Just remember that whenever we talk about security and motorcycle touring, the goal should be to keep the honest people honest, because professional thieves will always find a way to get your stuff if they want it.

One item I keep on hand is a seven foot locking cable which is useful to lock down my bags as well as a jacket and a pair of pants if I want to do a little sight seeing in an area. For the garments, simply thread the cable through the sleeve of the coat and one leg of the pants. When you're done, roll the cables up and stash it into it's little case which is about the size of your palm.

Chapter Four

Motorcycle Stuff

Here we'll cover the basics you need to have while you're on the road. If it's domestic travel you have in mind, this is about all you'll need. If you're planning to go abroad then a fat tool kit, lots of spare parts and extra inner tubes are recommended.

Chain Oil/Wax & Rag

Most chains need light lubrication about every 500 miles. Sure, modern day o-ring chains are internally lubricated, but a coat of oil or wax keeps all those little O rings shiny, and ensures your chain doesn't get all rusty after a little rain ride.

Store the oil or wax together in a plastic freezer bag along with a rag you'll use to remove the excess when you spray the chain.

My favorite chain lube is made by Motorex, Formula 622. It comes in a large seventeen ounce can as well as a small two ounce size which can be refilled from the large spray can just by docking the two together. The two ounce can packs light and compact.

I mentioned earlier how I used to forget stuff I needed all the time before creating a list to pack with. Chain oil was one. I had a ton of little bottles of 3 in 1 oil around the house I had picked up along the way on various trips as a result. If you forget your chain lube, or run out while you're on the road, get some sort of wax or silicone based lubricant and stay away from WD40 which is actually more of a solvent/penetrant, than a lubricator when it comes to motorcycle chains.

Tire Gauge *SR!*

Way too many bikes that arrive for service at dealers show up with their tires under inflated. The majority of us don't monitor our tire pressure as closely as we  should, which should be just about every day you ride. It's amazing how fast it can change.

There are many kinds of tire pressure gauges. The dial type, digital and pen style are just a few. The important thing is that you carry one with you when you ride and check your tire pressure at least weekly – more often if you're on a road trip.

When you're on the road a slow leak can cause you to lose just enough pressure overnight to land you on your butt when you enter into that first low speed twisty in the morning.

More to the point, a slow unmonitored leak allows a tire to gradually lose pressure until the carcass gets overheated and is damaged, and that can lead to a catastrophic failure even if you pump the tire back up to pressure.

There are a gazillion tire pressure gauges on the market. You don't need an expensive one when you travel, just one that's accurate. At home I have an expensive dial pressure gauge which I know to be accurate within about 5%. I just compare my small hand held digital one to be sure they're close and pack the hand held. Inexpensive "pencil-type" gauges have proven surprisingly accurate in magazine tests.

CruzTools makes a nice digital hand held gauge that runs on a CR2032 watch battery. It's likely it will never peter out during its lifetime since it has an automatic shut off, but if it did, I could easily find a new battery at the next big box convenience store along the route.

The EZ Air dial tire gauge made by Best Products works in line with their Cycle Pump making it handy to monitor the air pressure in your tires as you pump them up. You just attach the gauge to your valve stem, then add air to the gauge until the dial reads at the pressure you want, and remove the gauge.

Tool Kit SR!

Having the right tools at the right time is critical when You've got a problem on the road. Some manufacturers no longer provide a tool kit. And those OEM kits that ship with bikes are often cheaply made and incomplete.

I make a point of getting the tools out and taking an inventory before a long trip. I replace the tools that appear whimpy, and add any tools I might need on the road.

CruzTools makes a number of replacement tool kits for both Metric and SAE models. They come in two flavors – a less expensive off-shore version and a 100% American Made option.

Replacement tool kits like this one from CruzTOOLS are readily available and a nice way to up the quality of an OEM kit.

If you bought your motorcycle used, be sure it has a tool kit and that it is complete before you leave on a long trip. It's a good idea to store your tools in a divided fabric roll, to keep the metal from clanking together and rusting.

Tire Repair Kit *SR!*

When looking over your tools, consider what you'd do if you had a tire puncture far from civilization. Repair kits and battery-powered pumps don't take up a lot of space but will get you going again when you get a flat..

I recommend your kit include patches and glue, plugs and string if you're running radials, a pump and few large pieces of old inner tube rubber if you need to patch a large slice or hole from the inside of the tire.

I carry my own kit that I culled from a trip to the auto parts section at one of those big box stores. It includes tools, patches and parts to repair both tube and tubeless tires. Sometimes that winds up being my own, other times it's another stranded rider. The kit includes two CruzTools TirePro tire irons, which are long for good leverage. It also includes extra valves, a valve removal tool, latex gloves and hand wipes. Bicycle repair kits and levers just don't have what it takes to handle motorcycle flats.

Tire Pump

Carry a tire pump on your motorcycle? Sounds a little like overkill right? Until the moment arises when you need it.

You might be in the middle of nowhere miles from the nearest air compressor. You could go the cheap route and carry a bicycle hand pump. Try that for a while and you'll see what a pain they are to get the pressure up to 20 or 30 pounds in a motorcycle tire.

There are a number of 12 volt portable pumps on the market. You can get cheap pumps in space-wasting plastic housings for about twenty bucks at Kmart and auto parts stores.

My choice, however, is the Cycle Pump from Best Products. The pump is encased in a metal box making it far more durable than most store-bought pumps of this type. It's also made in America. These two factors put its price tag at about $100 making it five times more expensive than the el cheapo versions from Mr. Wall and Mr. K, but reliability factors in high here. The other thing I like about the pump is its ability to connect with its compatible EZ-Air gauge so you can monitor inflation live.

The Cycle Pump and EZ Air gauge work together for a live reading when inflating your tires.

Does everyone in the group need to take a

pump along? Hardly. If one or two riders in your touring group have a pump that's probably all you'll need.

Spare Bulbs & Fuses

Imagine this scenario – you're 500 miles from home, 100 miles from an auto parts store and your headlight bulb goes dead right at sundown. You've never replaced the bulb and don't even know what size the replacement is, but you need to get to your destination 100 miles from where you are. Yikes.

When was the last time you replaced your front headlight bulb? If the answer is never, then make a point of doing it at home sooner than later – it's a good exercise to go through before you hit the road. You never know how easy or hard it will be until you try it once.

Do you know what size spare headlight bulb you need to carry? Many people don't and you may be surprised to find out yours isn't stocked on the shelf at the Acme Auto Supply store in Nowhere, USA. You're much better off identifying at home what the replacement bulb is and purchasing one before you go.

Ditto for a replacement blinker and tail light as well as a few of each different fuse your bike requires.

Store all your spares in their own tote bag. Wrap tape around the packaging the lights come in. If you don't the backing paper will eventually separate from the plastic front panel from getting jostled around so much and cut the bulbs loose inside your tote bag. It's important to keep those bulbs cushioned, and not touch the glass with bare hands.

Spare Keys

Ever locked your trunk key in your luggage? Probably not since a lot of hard luggage requires the key to lock it as well as unlock it. But keys get used a lot along the road, and eventually one is bound to get weak and break as you insert it into the ignition, gas cap, helmet lock or storage compartment door. You could also simply misplace your key, like leaving it in the booth at the restaurant the night before or something like that.

A spare key takes up little room and you can simply slip one into your jacket pocket. Better yet, hide the spare key in some hidden crevice of the bike so it's always with the bike and not in the jacket you didn't wear today.

Spare Stuff – Spare bulbs, fuses and keys are a good idea for any trip.

I prefer OEM keys from the manufacturer over those sold at the locksmith. They cost a bit more, but usually are made with tougher metal. You can order them from your dealer, and if you provide your key number, sometimes you can get them pre-cut.

Locksmiths carry a small thin barbed tool that works great for extracting a broken key from a lock. They say they're not supposed to sell them to regular consumers like you and me, but if you can get ahold of one, they're a godsend when you're in a pinch with a broken key stuck in a lock.

Packing Light *Packing Right*

Chapter Five

Clothing to Pack

In this section we'll discuss the clothing to pack for the ride, whether a day ride or overnight.

Raingear

Raingear is a great item to carry whether it's raining or not. Besides keeping you dry it can also help you stay warm by keeping the wind off your riding gear allowing you to maintain existing body heat for a longer time.

If you've ever been caught in a rainstorm, only to find your raingear is leaking, then you know the importance of having good quality raingear. There's a lot of raingear on the market today. Some of it works, but unfortunately some of it leaks after just a few uses – usually the less expensive product.

The seat of the pants is often the first to go. This becomes especially evident if you have a pocket shape to your seat, common on cruiser bikes and often a preferred choice when a rider has a seat custom built by an upholstery house. When selecting raingear, look for models where the seams in the crotch can be accessed. This will allow you to re-tape the seam should it open up and leak. Seam tape and seam coatings can be purchased at better outdoor gear and fabric stores. Some raingear has an interior liner in the pant that does not allow for easy access to the seams – stay away from those.

Look for raingear that fits closely to you. Most brands of raingear designed by motorcycle clothing manufacturers do this. Some people put on loose fitting raingear, often made by an outdoor gear company, only to turn into sails when the wind comes up. The other issue with raingear designed by outdoor clothing manufacturers is that it's designed to do things like fish or hike in, not drive into the wind at sixty miles an hour all day long. Before you buy a set of raingear, try it on, sitting on your bike in riding position.

Raingear does a great job of helping you stay warm when it's cold out. Newer models of raingear have good venting systems that allow air to mildly circulate through the suit keeping you from getting moldy, but not so much that you're expelling body heat at an alarming rate, so you can stay warmer longer. I often ride on summer mornings with my raingear on to beat the dawn chill, then take it off when things warm up.

If it's raining out, be sure to slip the sleeve openings over the gauntlet of your glove. This will keep water coming down your arms from finding its way into your gloves.

There are those who believe that because their riding jacket and pants are said to be waterproof they don't need raingear. They believe they will actually stay dry when mother nature goes to town with a good rainstorm and later learn the hard way.

I recall a trip from the Columbia River Gorge to Paradise Lodge at Mount Rainier. I was traveling with four other journalists. The one with the Aerostich jacket and pants was sure he didn't need extra raingear because he had paid hundreds of dollars for his gear and it was reputed to be waterproof. It was not. Ditto for the guy with the European textile riding jacket and pants. These two guys were soaked from head to toe by the time we reached the lodge after riding two hours in an inch-an-hour rainfall. The other three of us had PVC coated rain suits on over our riding gear. We were dry as a bone – now imagine that.

Spare Gloves

Return to my sermon on gloves in chapter two for a refresher on glove tips if you need it.

When you carry spare gloves, make sure they aren't the same thickness as the ones you'll be wearing when you start the ride. Carry various thicknesses of gloves so you have options based on the weather.

When packing your spare gloves, make sure you can access them easily, don't pack them at the bottom of your luggage where you'll have to tear things apart to get to them.

Rain Hat/Sun Visor SR!

Now that mankind has put holes all over the ozone, it's advisable to carry a hat or sun visor whenever you ride so you can keep the sun off your head when you're not wearing a helmet..

The hat I like the best is the Seattle Sombrero made by Outdoor Research. It features a full brim, Gore-Tex in the crown so it won't leak and a chin cord so it won't blow off in the wind.

I wear it when it's sunny and when it's raining. It's handy when I want to load the gear onto my bike in the rain, but don't want to wear my helmet just yet. It's handy when I stop to take photographs because the brim flips up allowing me to bring my camera to my face without the hat getting in the way.

I can also crumble it up, and it always returns to its shape. It's very easy to pack and fits around other items in my tank bag.

Cold Weather Vest *SR!*

When it comes to cold weather, the worst thing you can let happen is to allow your core to get cold. All heat that emanates to the extremities of your body (your arms, hands, feet, legs and head) comes from your core where your heart is. If this area of your body chills down your next stop is hypothermia. You don't want this to happen.

A fleece vest comes in handy when you need to keep the core warm. It insulates the heat that's coming off your body in a big way and allows you to better manage your body heat on cold rides. They don't take up much room in your luggage and can really be a life saver.

The one I use is made by Techniche. The vest includes 8 pockets you can slip heat packs into. Four on the front and four on the back.

Evaporative Cooling Vest SR!

Now let's assume it's summer. The core now gets overheated and that spells heat stroke. There are all kinds of ways people try to cool down when it's hot during a motorcycle ride. But a tank top t-shirt is not the answer. Hot wind hitting a hot body just heats you up faster.

Water is a factor when it comes to cooling. If you can get your skin wet around the core, your body can transfer excess heat away from itself much more easily. That's why we perspire in the first place. In my earlier motorcycling days we used to stop and soak down long sleeve t-shirts, place them onto our bodies wet and ride. Boy did that feel great, except that after an hour the shirts were totally dry.

Today I carry an evaporative cooling vest. When dry it only weighs six ounces and packs very small. I pack it in a #1 size dry bag. When the temperature goes up, I pull out at the next gas station, fill the bag with water with the vest inside. After a few minutes the vest takes on about two thirds of a gallon of water. I put the vest on under my jacket and can ride an entire afternoon without having to recharge it.

Your t-shirt gets wet which is fine, because you want to create that transport ability for your excess body heat. When you find yourself headed for cooler weather, like a mountain pass, remove the vest about 30 minutes before you arrive so you can dry out your shirt. You don't want to head into a cooler mountain pass with a wet shirt on.

The vest style I prefer is with a collar and no sleeves. I've tried the vests with sleeves but the experience has been too cold when riding in the 90's. It's an odd feeling and one I find unpleasant. The sleeveless vests are also less expensive and pack smaller.

There are other products on the market said to cool you down. I've seen neck ties that take an hour to fully hydrate and dry out just as fast. These neck ties do little to cool your core down. Ditto for wet do-rags, wet bandanas and the like. If your core is cool, then your neck and head will be too, because the blood going to those places is not overheated. There's no need to carry several different cooling devices, a vest will do the trick all on its own.

Chapter Six

Personal Stuff

We're all individuals and we all need certain things on the road. What's covered here are the basics, but for those of you who need insulin, have other prescriptions, or have a few other favorites you like to pack like makeup or a hairdryer, add them to the list here.

Reading Glasses SR!

For those of us who would otherwise starve being unable to read a menu at the next roadhouse, it's easy to get away with small reading glasses on the road. The local drug store has a lot of options in all powers and many are small. The latest are road readers, a small set of reading glasses that slip into a compact protective case.

Several years ago I came across a touring set of eyewear with interchangeable lenses from Global Vision called C-2000s, featuring five sets of lenses you could swap into the frames. Then they took it two steps further when they offered a bi-focal option in a clear lens and a kit that had bi-focal lenses in clear and smoke. Now that's nice if you need to read your GPS and other instruments on a bright sunny day while traveling.

Sunscreen *SR!*

Don't fool around with sunshine. A motorcycle ride is not the place to work on your tan. Use sunscreen with an SPF of 30 or higher

I still have not figured out how it happens, but even my forehead shows signs of being in the sun when I travel, and I've got a full-face helmet on! But the one thing I have learned about sunscreens is that lotions are messy. They leave a residue wherever they go; for motorcyclists that means in our helmets and our jacket sleeve interiors.

Even the ones that say they are non-greasy turn out to be – greasy! We've tried a few that aren't. Sierra Summits and Smart Shield don't hang around on the surface of your skin too long and provide a sun protection factor (SPF) 30. They also don't sting much if you get them into your eyes because they utilize zinc oxide as the major ingredient and not the other chemicals that tend to sting.

Sun screen in the eyes stings like the dickens. Don't you think!? There's two reasons we get sunscreen into our eyes. With lotions, when things heat up they tend to find their way down the epidermis and into our tear ducts. The other is that when we go to get something out of our eye, like some crusty sleep, dirt or dust, the mere act of touching the area carries anything nearby on our skin into our eyes. Be careful how you touch this area when you're wearing sunscreen.

Foot Powder *SR!*

In the spirit of having a comfortable ride, use a little foot powder in your socks and toss a little directly into your boots before you ride. The typical foot powder will help to manage moisture in your socks all day. Get some with antibacterial properties. There are two advantages to having it. It will stave off typical athlete's foot, but, more importantly, if your boots get wet inside from going through a puddle or river crossing, you can stave off some serious itching.

I was once riding through Oregon when I came across a twenty foot long river crossing. I made it across without dumping the bike, but it was deep enough to get some water into my boot. I still had another eight hours of riding to do that day. Had I not had foot powder I don't know how I would have managed the itch that would have otherwise tortured me all day.

The foot powder I like best was actually designed to be a skin powder. Anti Monkey Butt powder proves itself as a great foot powder, and I've also used it to initiate scabbing on open cuts.

Skin Lubricants *SR!*

As you ride in the saddle all day long, the first contact on your skin is your underwear. With seams that are constantly pressing into your skin, now and then you need to slide your butt around to negotiate more comfort. But if you're perspiring, your underwear is less likely to comply to your desired adjustment and your time in the saddle gets more uncomfortable and begins to cause an underlying fatigue.

A few guys that rode bicycles figured this out and created a product called Chamois Butt'r. The product is a skin lubricant that keeps clothing from sticking to your skin and allows you to change positions and effectively negotiate a better comfort level.

Lip Balm

I carry lip balm and use it when my lips get dry. I don't use it everyday because I've found if I apply lip balm on a regular basis, the skin rescinds it's own moisture-making requirements, and I become a slave to the stuff. Get the kind with a good SPF rating so you protect yourself from UV rays.

Toothbrush/Toothpaste

The smaller the better. You've seen the little travel versions that pack up small and you'll find small tubes of toothpaste located in the travel size section of better drug stores. Or, when your big tube of toothpaste at home is almost all used up, save the tail end for travel.

Dental Floss

Did you know only fifteen percent of the North American population flosses their teeth each day? I've got food traps big enough to get an extra meal from each day so it's imperative I clean them out daily. Maintain healthy teeth at home and on the road and you're less likely to go see the country dentist when you get to Bumpkinville.

Pills & Pain Relievers

Here's another one of those things I used to forget to pack until I started keeping a good packing list. I'd often find myself in the mini mart buying little packs of ibuprofen fending off hip pain, old age or otherwise.

Whatever pills you're carrying on the road, I highly recommend you use those little cotton balls in the bottles to minimize the wear and tear as you bump around from the interstate to the not so great tertiary road.

As you get older and older, you'll probably need to carry various prescriptions and supplements with you as you travel. If you don't need to prove what's in the bottle, you can repack a supply of pills in those divided plastic pill boxes (free at some drugstores) and save a lot of space.

As for prescriptions and labels on bottles in general, after those containers rub around enough all over each other in a mesh bag, the labels are going to wear on them. If that information on them is important to you, put a layer or two of clear Scotch tape over them to preserve it.

Allergy Stuff

Several years back I began developing some very unpleasant allergic reactions to pollens. I tried to whip it with over-the-counter drugs, but those made me feel spacey and drowsy. Not how you want to feel when you ride a motorcycle.

If you have developed some allergies, but have yet to see a doctor about it, make an appointment before your next ride and have them interview you about it. There are some great prescription medicines that have fewer side effects and make the difference between a lousy time and a good one. In my case I have both eye drops and a nasal product I use if need be. I don't use them unless I have symptoms.

Nail Clippers

I carry a large one so I can do both my fingers and toes. I'm not fond of attempting to cut my nails with the scissors in my multi-purpose knife so I go with a separate set of nail clippers. Some of the larger ones have an inverse crescent which cuts the nail without splintering, leaving no hang nails. Use the file in your Leatherman to finish off.

Chapter Seven

Information & Currency

Having the right information when you ride means less hassle with the police if you're stopped, and easier border crossings if you're heading out of the country.

Drivers License

I keep my driver's license in a separate place when I'm not riding and have to transfer it every time I ride. It's on my list so I don't forget.

Be sure yours is current and has a motorcycle endorsement. If you're traveling without a motorcycle endorsement I'm sure you're already aware that you can be fined severely, but did you know it's also a State's responsibility to take possession of your motorcycle until you can prove you're endorsed to ride it again? Now this is the extreme and it almost never happens, but if you're caught without an endorsement it is the officer's option to have your bike towed to the yard of their choice.

In many states, the extra money you pay for a motorcycle endorsement is used to fund rider education for the next league of motorcyclists. I happily pay my twenty five dollars every five years so we can continue training riders at a subsidized rate in the state where I live.

Proof of Insurance

Some states require liability insurance, others do not. If you don't have it and plan to ride to another state, you better look into what their laws are. In Washington State, where I live, motorcyclists are not required to carry insurance. But in Idaho and Oregon they are, and I know many a rider who has been fined heavily and told to 'go home' by local law enforcement in those states.

If you are stopped by an officer, you'll need to produce both your drivers license and bike registration—which should be signed by the owner. If you're riding a borrowed bike, you also should have a letter from the owner giving you permission to be riding it.

Review your insurance policy yearly and add or subtract to the coverages based on the value of your bike and how much liability you think you will need, say to cover the medical expenses of a small child who grabbed your header pipe, or a silver-haired pedestrian in intensive care after you clipped her in a crosswalk. Scary thought, but in some states liability is not a required coverage.

I keep my proof of insurance, along with my registration buried deep under my seat in a plastic freezer bag. That way if I get pulled over the officer gets to wait for me to basically unload the entire bike so I can get the seat up. If it's raining they especially feel sorry for putting you up to the trouble – most of the time.

Bike Registration

Make sure your motorcycle registration is current. Again, I bury my registration deep under the seat in a plastic freezer bag to keep it dry.

If you've recently purchased a different bike, make a point of checking the actual frame number against the number on your registration certificate. An error in the number might mean your license or insurance is invalid. While you're at it, check your license plate tab and make sure it's current too. Thieves steal these things all the time, even off motorcycles.

Passport/ID Card

If you plan on crossing the border from America, you'd better pack your passport. And it's surprising how many people don't. Even after 911, I entered into Canada with a business associate who thought he'd be fine with just his driver's license. We spent an extra half hour at the border going in, and another extra half hour coming back to the U.S.

Membership Cards

AAA, AMA, Subway and so on. Pack the cards you'll need. Just make a point of checking your membership and discount cards, and pack the ones you'll need. If you have emergency towing insurance, be sure you understand the rules, and have the telephone number handy. If you need to rent a car, it helps to have your group discount number with you.

If you have AAA, you have no towing coverage for your motorcycle unless you opt for the recreational vehicle option each year you renew. AMA has a similar option. Subway sandwiches does not, but remember the card if you're into their points game.

Cash

Cash is king. It's accepted just about everywhere (just about – more on that in a moment). I typically like to keep about $100 cash on me when I ride so I can cover little expenses like snacks, water and fuel. It's a good idea to make sure you have more than five dollars before you hit the road each day. ATMs are all over the place in the US and Canada, but the withdrawal charge is the same for $3 or $300, so it's best to withdraw cash in bigger chunks. Better yet do your withdrawals when making purchases at the grocery store where often times there is no fee.

Credit Cards

Credit cards make stopping for gas much simpler. You can save two trips into the service station cashier and be on your way much sooner by just slipping your card into the pump.

I said cash is accepted *almost* anywhere. There's a new game going on in petrol land. Seems the station owners are leasing the onsite mini marts out to other individuals, separating the sales inside from the fuel sold at the pump. Some cashiers will say you can't pay for your gas inside with cash or credit and that if you want fuel, you'll need to buy it with a credit card outside.

There are a few people still left in America who refuse to use credit cards, or can't anymore because of something in their past. This 'credit only' situation could be a serious problem in the middle of nowhere. If you don't travel with a credit card, gas up at your own risk, or simply travel with someone who has one so they can act as your surrogate credit extension.

Before we go any further I must admit that more than once I have left the house without my wallet and had to scrounge up money along the way. These days I keep a few 20s and a credit card in one of your Nite Ize Multi Pock-It's holsters. Do the same and you'll have a backup should it happen to you.

Maps and Travel Guides *SR!*

Good maps can make for a great trip, bad maps can make for a lousy one. The more current and the more detailed the better.

I personally like the atlases and folding maps produced by Benchmark Maps, an Oregon cartography company that updates their maps every three years – and that includes dirt and gravel road updates as well. The maps are very detailed and are packed with recreational information for each state they cover. This is nice because it allows me to sightsee much better when I'm out and about.

I've moved away from the Rand MacNally Atlases and DeLorme Gazetteers. The updates don't happen often enough and the markings are all too often inaccurate. Like the time I went eight miles on a dirt road that was marked as paved in the Gazetteer. I was using a bike with

belt drive and my riding partner was on a sportbike. Yow.

And then there was the time I was using a map produced by King of the Road, a company that produces a lot of folding maps for the travel store market. The pass we planned to ride through was closed, but the map showed an alternate way around on a paved road. Instead the road ended about halfway along and turned into a campground. The map King of the Road produced had a 1998 copyright on it, but after a bit of research we discovered that had sourced this information from a 1946 USGS map that had a proposed road on it, but the road was never completed.

If you plan to carry an atlas, consider a durable atlas case. SR! sells a premium waterproof see-through case designed by Cycoactive that holds an atlas and can handle a few more things if need be. I strap it to the outside of my luggage so I can view the state map on the back cover without having to remove it from the case.

Alternatively, it's not a crime to snip pages out of your book of maps and insert into a tank bag window. After all, you'll probably want to replace your maps every few years with more current information. Some people buy two copies of the same atlas. One to keep at home and the other to tear apart as needed.

Paper and Pen

As a journalist, I'm pretty good about packing paper and pens. I'm usually the guy who ponies one up when another rider needs one. Then I lose that one, and I resort to one of a few spares I keep in my luggage.

I've found a lot of people never pack one. But inevitably you'll need one to copy down some travel information, write a reminder for later, or get an important phone number or email for people you meet along the way.

A small address notepad travels pretty well. There's rarely a need to carry a large pad or loose sheets of 8 ½ x 11 when you're traveling. They're bulky and get crumpled up during the ride, whereas the pad packs away easily.

If you have small pockets in your riding jacket, you can stuff the writing pad and pen inside a waterproof bag and stow where they are easy to find.

Phone List/Roster

If you're traveling with a group, everyone should exchange cell phone numbers and any other important contact information before the ride begins. My preferred way to do a group ride is to let everyone spread out – way out. The more people spread out, the less chance for accidents.

If you're on a tour you should have cell numbers for everyone in your group as well as the tour operator, key people involved with the trip back at home and hotels and motels along the route. It's nice to know you can spread a group two hours apart from itself during the riding day and everyone can still get in touch with one another if they need to.

Tickets & Passes

It's fun to tour far away and see a show at some point during the trip. In Washington State for example there are several outdoor amphitheaters that are smack in the middle of nowhere. It would be a shame to arrive without your tickets.

And now all the national and state park agencies have got us paying fees to enter *OUR* parks, offering annual passes to those who go frequently. If you plan to go in and out of these parks more than five times a year, it's often worth the expense to buy the pass. Just don't leave it at home in your SUV where you placed it on that last hiking trip.

Maxi Scooters are becoming popular and make for great touring bikes when called upon to do so. This one is loaded for a multi day trip utilizing one 80 liter luggage case and the 70 liters of storage under the seat. The photo was taken at the Stonehenge replica in Washington State.

Chapter Eight

Gadgets & Otherwise

If we were going on a motorcycle tour fifty years ago, most of the items listed here would not have been packed into our bags. But it's different today and technology has afforded us better navigation tools, better communication tools and smaller-sized gear to record our trip as we ride.

GPS & Mounts *SR!*

The GPS. There are those who say you don't need one and those who say they would never tour far from home without one. It all depends on who you are, I guess. I have no qualms with people using GPS.

GPS units are not cheap if you buy one of good quality and the proper software to run for your riding situation. All in all, for a good GPS and software to tour in America, you'll spend about $1,000. That's a high price to pay to have a gadget tell you where you are. Hopefully you'll discover the other 999 things they do and make it a useful part of your riding.

On the highway I seldom use one unless I want to navigate a new area I have not ridden. When I get off-road on a dual sport ride it becomes a critical part of my navigation strategy. While I could use a decent paper atlas to guide me it means having to access that atlas at every junction to ensure I make the right turn in the right place. I don't have time to keep pulling out an atlas or maps as I'm riding off-road. If I've pre-routed my ride, either on or off the pavement, the GPS greatly enhances my ability to navigate seamlessly as I ride. And if I decide to take a side trip, I can always turn off the pre-routed navigation and just have a look at the map to locate a place to get back on the route when I decide to do so.

The best place I found to get a GPS is through REI. As an REI member I get 10% back on everything I buy there each year. In the case of the Garmin model and software I purchased for $700 that means I got back $70. Garmin also offered a rebate of $50 on my purchase so I saved a total of $120. Garmin does not honor rebates when the product is purchased through an online auction or non-franchised dealers, so what seems like a deal isn't so much so in the end, especially if you need service later as I did.

A Seattle company, RAM, produces the highest quality mounts that I've found. Their mounts have the least moving parts and are more durable than similar European models costing four times as much. RAM mounts can be purchased at better boat and marine stores. They are priced low enough I didn't mind buying a mount for each of my bikes so I can swap my GPS between them. The RAM mounts are well designed with the key points rubber mounted to reduce vibration.

My GPS model runs on two AA batteries. Over the years, manufacturers have learned to build better-quality cases realizing that it's not just people with cars, or hikers using their products. It used to be that batteries in a GPS on a motorcycle could be bad news because of the way they jump around, but today the design has compensated for that and it's much less of an issue.

Pre-route your ride at home, upload it to your GPS and don't forget to send the maps along with the upload. To be able to pick up portions of the same route heading home, you may need to reverse the route on your computer and upload it with a different name.

Camera and Accessories

Imagine touring 25 years ago with a 35mm camera, three lenses and a bunch  of film. Well – so much for having room in your luggage for anything else. Today small digital cameras that fit in a shirt pocket can take excellent photographs at resolutions high enough for print publishing.

While I do own a 35mm digital and all the big lenses, I normally only travel with a small Nikon pocket camera. When you see a scene you want to capture, your camera needs to be instantly accessible—perhaps in a jacket pocket or stored in your tank bag in a Multi Pock-Its holster.

I also take along extra batteries and a spare memory card in case I run out of juice or memory. If you plan to be out for several days or longer, remember to bring a battery charger too.

Cell Phone

It's as much a convenience as it is a survival tool. With modern cell service you can call ahead to a restaurant or motel, or you can call for help if you have a mechanical issue or go down in the middle of nowhere. That is if you have the right provider.

There's a lot of competition in the cell phone market. Over a dozen companies in one state may be vying for your dollars teasing you with free phones, free minutes or free upgrades. None of that matters when you're in the middle of nowhere. At that point the only thing that matters is making a connection, so you must consider the true calling area of a cell service provider and be certain they own that network and are not just piggybacking onto someone else's.

Allow me to step upon my soapbox for a moment…

I've used Sprint PCS for about five years. I've never been impressed with their calling area, but stuck with them as they grew. When I discovered friends with Verizon making calls from 7,500 feet off a barren plateau in the middle of the high dessert, 100 miles from the nearest town I contacted Sprint PCS and requested better coverage. They put me on a program to access Verizon's network. After that I would make a call in a far away place, a recording would say "Welcome to the Verizon Network" then I'd hear a busy signal. Are you getting my point?

If you plan to tour extensively on your motorcycle in America, make sure you're on the best network, whatever that may be.

Spare Batteries

AA batteries are my friends. They run my flashlight, camera, shaver and GPS when I travel. I've purposely selected gadgets that run on AA batteries to keep down the variation of batteries needed when I travel. By having these four items on the same size battery I only have to take an extra two or four out with me. If I get in a pinch, AA batteries are readily available along the route.

When packing them, rubber band them together to keep them from sloshing around in the mesh bag you stow them into. That way when you need them you don't have to play hide-and-seek to find them.

The only AA batteries I carry are rechargeable 2700mAh NiMH (Nickel-Metal Hydride) batteries which I purchase at my local pro camera shop. They hold a big charge and are immune to the "memory" effects common in Nickel

Cadmium (Ni-CAD) batteries, which eventually make them useless after a number of chargings. They also allow me to keep the environment clean by never having to dispose of them.

During a multi-day dual sport ride, I watched another rider go through 15 pair of non-rechargeable Duracell batteries he had bought in quantity at Costco just for our ride. It was unnecessary weight and a useless waste and burden on the environment.

Battery Chargers

We've already talked about remembering to bring your battery charger for your camera (few digital cameras run on AA batteries anymore so I've noted it separately here), but remember to bring the charger for your cell phone and AA batteries too. The smaller they are, the better.

I carry a one-hour charger for my Nickel-Metal Hydride batteries. I don't usually have 16 hours to wait for a charge from a standard one, but an hour usually means I can charge the batteries while I'm stopped for lunch somewhere or overnight when I stop for the day. I've used one hour chargers on Nickel-Metal Hydride batteries for several years and not noticed any loss of charge capacity. On the other hand you can ruin a set of Nickel Cadmium batteries very quickly with a one hour charger.

Chapter Nine

Survival Basics

Water and first aid are two things you need to consider before you ride. Dehydration and not being ready for an accident situation are actually pretty common mistakes. Don't learn it the hard way. Make sure you've got water and a first aid kit with you.

Water

Since most of our body consists of water, you need to drink a lot of it everyday – even the days you ride your motorcycle. Rain or shine, you'll need to replace all the water you're expelling via perspiration and urination. Dehydration on a motorcycle can show up in no time at all if it's hot and you're not taking in what you're losing. It's not pretty when it strikes. Drink water all day long. Drink lots several days before, too.

The simplest way I've found to carry water is to buy it in plastic bottles at the grocery store or gas station mini mart. I despise tap water if it's not filtered so I'm always happy to pay for water.

There are those who would rather fill up a plastic sports bottle and for them that's fine. Sports bottles are thicker than regular bottled water containers. Therefore they weigh a bit more and take up more space. Katadyne now makes a sports bottle with a built in filter.

My dual sport friends have asked me why I don't wear a CamelBak unit on my back. I do fine getting water into me during stops and don't feel the need to have to take a drink while in motion. And if you want to know a nasty flavor for water, just drink out of a CamelBak after the water has been in there for several hours.

I once spoke to a manufacturer's rep for CamelBak at the Outdoor Retailer show in Salt Lake City. I mentioned to him I didn't like the way the water tasted from a CamelBak after several hours and he agreed. Then I asked him if there was any new technology that was going to change that. He responded "whoever can figure that one out is going to make us all rich." So for now I'm sticking with bottled water.

First Aid Kit

Finally we've reached the first aid kit section. We've saved so much space in our luggage so far that now we actually have room to stow one inside.

There's a lot of information about what and why to carry certain items. It's a good idea to spend some time online researching the various kits available and then selecting or creating the right one for you.

Poison Extractor

If you're traveling anywhere that poisonous snakes live, consider packing a Sawyer Extractor. There's no need to cut the skin as there is no scalpel involved, instead the unit is a pump that can be used with one hand.

They're reusable and you can also use them for mosquito bites, bee stings, scorpion stings and other critter retaliation. You can pick one up at REI and other better outdoor stores.

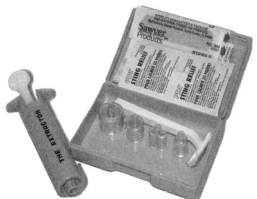

The best medicine for a snake bite by far is to get the victim to a hospital as soon as possible so they can get anti-venom. It helps if you can identify what kind of snake it was, too.

Space Blanket

If you wind up in a situation where you or your riding partner is going into shock from an accident situation, a space blanket will help maintain body heat until help arrives. These are thin little mylar sheets that are big enough to wrap around you. They come folded up and take up very little space.

Here's a tip if you're going somewhere really warm. I once was hiking in Hawaii on an overnight trip. For the sake of less space, and knowing the nighttime temperature was going to be a warm seventy five degrees, I left my sleeping bag at home and slept with only a space blanket on a sleeping pad. It worked as I was warm all night. Even better I didn't have to carry the extra weight of a sleeping bag since I was suffering having trashed my left knee during a fall the day before.

Chapter Ten

Little Helpers

I keep a mesh bag loaded with all my little helpers. These are the things I use when I need to do a quick fix or maintain what I have.

Optical Cleaners & Enhancers SR!

We sell a lot of eyewear in our online store. Keeping it at its highest optical visibility is critical to reducing fatigue and enjoying the ride. Dirty or scratched lenses distract a rider from paying attention to the road. And then you also need to

consider your face shield and wind screen if you have one on your bike – imagine that, you could be looking through three different clear surfaces before you actually see the road, so the cleaner they are the better.

I've tested a lot of cleaning products, and the one I've found to be the best is called Novus 1 Plastic Clean and Shine. Under continual use, the product did not deteriorate the surface of eyewear, face shields and wind screens. Others, like Meguiars plastic cleaner and Windex do. In fact Windex is one of the worst things you can apply to plastic, because it begins peeling off the surface and causes a haze. It's designed to be used on glass.

Another demon for plastic is the scrubber on the back side of the squeegee at the gas station. Use your common sense and never rub your face shield with a scrubber on a squeegee which was designed to be used on glass – not plastic. You'll scratch your face shield in no time.

I tend to change my face shield as often as necessary, because eventually we all wind up with scratches that are too big to remove with a mild abrasive that won't deteriorate the optical clarity of plastics. For me that's at least once a year and sometimes twice if I'm doing a lot of off-road travel.

What you use to rub and dry your eyewear with is critical too. Get yourself a nice micro-fiber cleaning cloth. Cotton fibers are too large and don't absorb dirt into the fabric as you rub, so a cotton towel can do more damage than good. Paper towels will do the most damage, and yet I've seen plenty of riders use them at the gas station.

I keep a small two ounce bottle of Novus 1 and a micro-fiber cleaning cloth in a freezer bag tucked into my tank bag. I wash the cloth each night I'm on the road.

I also carry a bottle of Nikwax Visor Proof which works well on the outside of face shields to bead water away for better visibility. How often you need to re-apply depends on how hard it's raining.

Fogging on the inside of the face shield is a problem especially when the humidity increases during rainfall. I've tried all the tricks like the Fog City, Pin Lock and other inserts. I don't care for them. When it's minimal I just lift my shield and let nature take its course. But – when it's really bad I use a shot of Scott Anti Fog cleaner which you can pick up at the ski shop.

Cable Ties

These little miracles have hundreds of uses; you just have to wait for the situation to arise. Carry at least ten eight-inch ties with you. You just never know when you'll use them. Here's a few times when riders have.

Frankenstein? After this bike hit the pavement, the owner used the auger tool like the one in a Leatherman to create holes and stitch the plastic back together with cable ties.

Scotty Sport Rider went down breaking an exterior plastic panel on his bike. It was hanging there with some critical wires attached to the backside that would have been left vulnerable if he broke off the plastic and tossed the panel. Instead he used a Leatherman tool to make small holes along each side of the break, and then zip tied the panel back together. Nice one, Scotty.

Gloria Goldwing once discovered a wire rubbing on the frame of her bike Using a zip tie she was able to secure it, eliminating the friction and an impending short circuit.

Snoring Bob was ready to turn in one night on the road. His riding partner reminded him to use a snoring strip before he went to bed so she could sleep too, but Bob didn't bring one – or did he? Bob took out a zip tie, trimmed it with the scissors on his Leatherman, backed it with a little duct tape, then placed it onto his nose and they both slept happily ever after.

You never know what you'll come up with for using a zip tie, but by having it on hand, it'll be there ready to serve no matter what the need is.

Duct Tape

There's always something you can put back together with duct tape. Most convenience stores sell small rolls of it, which are easier to pack than those big ones you see in the hardware store.

Flashlight *SR!*

My flashlight of choice is a Mag Lite with a Nite Ize LED Conversion like the one you see here. LED lights cost more, but the batteries last much longer and the bulb lasts far longer than other types too.

Even if you only plan to ride for the day, carry a small flashlight. You never know when you'll need to inspect an area of the bike that is not well lit, such as the inside of a motor part or the interior area of your frame.

Multi-purpose Tool SR!

I've already mentioned the Leatherman tool several times in the book, so you know it's my choice for a multi-purpose tool. Specifically the Leather Juice XE6, because it comes with a corkscrew and file, as well as all the other dozen blades, scissors and such.

Back in my youth the popular tools of choice to carry on road trips were Buck knives and Swiss Army knives. They were sort of useful, but the addition of pliers, a corkscrew, file, saw and four screwdriver bits in the Leatherman Juice makes it a handy all-in-one unit for my purposes.

Rubber Bands

A small assortment of both small and large are suggested here. For larger rubber bands, you can cut sections from an old inner tube.

Sewing Kit

A tear in your gear, tent or clothing can be patched up easily with a sewing kit. I like to have a needle in there where the eye opening is big enough I don't spend a lot of time futzing with threading it.

Sport Goop

Broken plastic can be a pain when you're riding. I've tried Super Glue and various dual epoxy systems, but the one I found to work the best has been Sport Goop, made by the people who make Goop for shoe repair. It holds together a wide variety of plastics and metals.

Keep it in a freezer bag in the event it becomes punctured along your journey.

Tear-Aid SR!

This nifty product includes a few different-sized strips of an elastic composition that will fix leaks in rain gear or tents, hold together body work, or patch up just about anything you might use a strip of plastic or rubber for.

Chapter Eleven

Overnight

In other countries like Europe and Canada motorcycle touring/camping is very common. In the United States it's more common toopt for the motel/hotel routine, otherwise known as credit card camping. It gets costly. Personally, I'd rather spend five hundred dollars on gear I can camp with for five years, than five hundred dollars for five nights in a hotel.

Would you believe? *There I am in the Columbia River Gorge with nothing more than two saddle bags, a tail bag and a tank bag. Inside is ALL my gear including camping stuff for a week on the road.*

Today camping gear has hit the point where some of us are actually more comfortable sleeping in a tent on a decent air mattress than finding out the mattress at the motel is hard or splotted with questionable stains; and even though we requested a non-smoking room, it still reeks from years of smoking, or smoke is wafting up from the room below..

I'm also finding that campgrounds are in better condition than ever. I once stayed in a private campground with a heated bathroom that was clean as a whistle. In fact, in 2004 I stayed in more than five such places. I have yet to stay at a campground in recent times that I wouldn't go back to again.

Let's consider the cost of camping in relation to staying in a motel. Touring Terry has planned out his trip schedule for next year. He's going to take a week off for a ride up and down the West Coast. He's also planning on going to a rally and taking a separate weekend trip through the mountains near his home. All in all he'll be on the road for ten nights. The cost of camping at the rally is included in his registration. The average economy motel costs $69 a night and a campground runs $15. If he stays in a motel all ten nights he'll pay $690 plus all applicable tax. If he pays the $15 for camping he'll only spend $105 (remember, camping at the rally was free so we're only calculating seven nights here). What's he gonna do with the $585 he saved? In the first year he can put it toward the cost of high- quality camping gear, in the second year he can put it in the bank in the "new bike" fund.

Camping gear also weighs about half of what similar stuff weighed just ten years ago. Lighter composites for tent poles, lighter yet more durable fabrics for construction and shedding excess weight in design have greatly reduced how much weight and space camping gear adds to your luggage. One less reason to look like that wooly mammoth.

But we all know that not everybody wants to camp, no matter how cost effective and serene it is. This chapter still holds some insight for you on what to pack in terms of clothing to wear when you're not on the bike. Just bear with the rest of us through the sleeping bag and tent sections.

Sleeping Bag SR!

The sleeping bag is a critical part of a good nights sleep so but don't pinch pennies here. As soon as you start pinching pennies on this item it gets heavier and won't keep you as warm. Look for an ultra-light down bag that has a temperature comfort rating into the high thirties. A bag like this should not weigh more than two pounds and should be about half as large when packed as its synthetic counterpart.

My bag of choice is the Hummingbird model made by the European company, Exped, and distributed in America through Outdoor Research of Seattle. As of this publication it was priced at $260. That's not cheap and neither should you be when it comes to your comfort on the road. Another bag I like is the Wicked Fast by Sierra Designs.

These are both down bags and you need to be aware that a down bag won't keep you warm if it gets wet (seems to work for ducks, but not for people – hmmm…). These bags are small enough you can pack them into a small #1 size dry bag.

Sleeping Pad *SR!*

Years ago when the Thermarest hit the scene it was all the rage. Finally we could get a little air between us and the ground and have a more comfortable sleep.

Zoom forward several decades. The folks at Exped have come up with the latest in technology when it comes to sleeping pads. It's called the DownMat. It's an air mattress that is filled with down. The dry bag it comes in serves two other purposes, one as the pump to fill it and another as your pillow when it's time to nod off. The inflated height of the mattress is three times that of a Thermarest, yet it rolls up to half the size. Because it has down inside, it retains your body heat inside the mattress keeping you warmer when it's cold out. It costs a mere $130.

Tent and Ground Cloth *SR!*

So far we've spent $390 on a sleeping bag and mattress. Next up we need a small lightweight tent.

An important thing to consider when buying a tent is size. Will you be traveling alone, or two up with your partner who will share space in the tent with you? Will you be bringing your gear into the tent at night?

I like to bring my gear into the tent at night, but typically I'm the only one in the tent. For me a two man tent works fine affording me the space I need to stow my luggage and still have room to sleep. One man tents just don't cut it because even if they have a vestibule extending off them, it's usually not large enough to stow most motorcycle luggage.

Weight is certainly a consideration. Two man tents range in weight from as light as three pounds to as heavy as ten pounds. For years, manufacturers have been creating tents where the rainfly is separate from the tent construction. That just means more weight today. There are finally tents coming on the market where the rainfly is part of the tent construction itself, shedding weight from the final mass.

Another way manufacturers have shed pounds is to incorporate a hiker's trekking pole into the design. The point being if a hiker is using a trekking pole already, why not use it to hold the tent up at night. That's fine for hikers, but for us motorcyclists we're going to need a tent that doesn't use that design since we don't carry anything near the size or shape as a trekking pole.

The tent I'm most fond of right now is the Baku created by Sierra Designs. It comes in one, two and three person versions, packs up

light and small and has all the sturdy hardware you'll need to erect it, which only takes about five minutes. With the Baku you don't mess around with a rainfly, because it's part of the construction. It breathes very well from both sides and has venting on the front and top for condensation. Price for the Baku 1 is $230, Baku 2 is $290 and the Baku 3 is $360.

All in all, I've got $680 invested into camping gear. That's the equivalent of 10 nights in an economy motel room after one year, and the next year I'm just keeping money in my pocket for other things.

When packing your tent, discard the sack the rig comes in and purchase a smaller compression bag. With the poles aside, place the tent and footprint into the compression bag and pull those straps tight so you free up precious space in your luggage.

But whether we're camping, or staying in motels we need some clothes to wear when we're not on the bike.

Pants & Shorts

We've talked a lot about packing lighter, synthetic fabrics and packing smaller. If you want to dramatically reduce nearly two pounds from your cargo take heed. A lot of riders pack a pair of denim jeans and a pair of shorts in their gear bag. The option is to pack a pair of lightweight cargo pants with zip off legs. In the case of say a 32/30 size the cargo pant weighs in at 13 ounces and stores about the size of a softball. The denim jeans and shorts on the other hand weigh 40 plus ounces and store in about the space of six softballs.

As was also pointed out earlier, the synthetics will dry in about twenty minutes in a typical dryer, whereas the denim products typically take about sixty minutes.

Spare Underwear and Socks

If you pack a tube of Woolite and give yourself 10 minutes each night, you could get away with only carrying one spare pair of socks and underwear. In fact, just for the sake of publicity, one person traveled through Europe without any underwear, instead cleaning his sole pair nightly in the hotel room and hanging it to dry overnight.

Pack what you need, but planning for laundry at least every other day will reduce the weight you carry and space needed. If you carry more than two changes you're probably carrying too much.

Street/Camp Shoes

Some riders think they'll just mosey around in their riding boots and don't need a spare set of shoes on the road. I prefer to get out of my boots and relax. I pack a lightweight pair of mesh shoes that breathe. They don't take up much space and make a relaxing difference at the end of the day.

Nylon Cord

Nylon cords don't take up much space and they're handy if you need to hang dry wet laundry, repair a tent line or need a little extra support for getting some last-minute gear onto the bike. Ten to twenty feet of 1/8 inch cord is enough.

Matches/Lighter

If you plan on lighting anything like a campfire or stove, then matches or a lighter come in handy. Pack them in a small freezer bag so they stay dry wherever they are.

Cooking Stove and Gear

If you plan to do your own meals then you'll need some decent cooking gear. Again, the lighter the better and don't skimp on quality. There's nothing like drooling for your morning coffee only to find out your stove is clogged.

Also, if you plan to tour at high altitudes, like above 4,000 feet, be sure you get a stove that performs at higher elevations like the one made by Jet Boil. Consult with the staff at the outdoor gear shop.

Plateware *SR!*

Lexan changed the face of camping plate ware in the 1980's, but it's gone one more step forward. A UK Company, Flatworld, has  come up with a line of high grade plastic plate ware that folds up flat. Called Orikaso, a set includes two cups, two bowls and two plates and takes up less space then an eight and a half by eleven notepad.

Chapter Twelve

Shower Kit *SR!*

While the shower kit is something that falls under the overnight category, it warrants it's own chapter due to the detail. The kit bag itself should be a small folding type that you can purchase at any outdoor gear shop. Surprisingly, most shops only carry one or two styles, so shop around before you buy. Some are too bulky for my taste. My kit bag of choice is a #3 Organizer made by Outdoor Research.

Plastic Bottles

Purchase a half dozen 1 ounce and a few 2 ounce bottles to use in your shower kit. You'll use them to store shampoo, laundry detergent and other liquids you carry.

An important thing to remember about plastic bottles is that as they rattle around on your ride, the tops tend to loosen up. Each time you use a plastic bottle be sure to tighten up the top so you don't wind up with shower gel, eyewear cleaner or sunscreen dripping in your luggage.

Bath Towel SR!

You don't need to pack a big towel for your trip. A thin microfiber towel will absorb as much water off your skin as a thick cotton towel. My towel weighs just three ounces; the comparable size cotton towel weighs 20 ounces and sucks up eight times the storage space. Microfiber towels dry fast too.

Wash Cloth *SR!*

Again, dump the cotton in lieu of a synthetic wash cloth that has an open weave on it. The open weave reduces weight and allows the cloth to dry out in a very short period of time. You can get these in the bath section of mass merchants like Target and WalMart. If you need something even smaller we carry a microfiber hand towel in our online store.

Hair & Body Soap

There is no need to carry large size bottles of hair shampoo, crème rinse or body wash on the road. Simply fill your one or two ounce bottles with some of your favorite shampoo, crème rinse and body wash from home. If you use bar soap at home, find some liquid soap you like. Bar soap can be messy when you're traveling and can also melt in extreme heat.

Deodorant

Don't ask me how I know this, but deodorant in stick form melts in extreme heat, too. Find a brand you like that's in a roll-on format and get a small bottle. I use Tom's of Maine, not just because it's natural, but because it also has my name in the brand.

Shaver

If you're a close shave guy then pack a stick and a few blades. Pick up a travel size bottle of shave crème for the road. You don't need to carry the regular larger ones.

I prefer electric and use a Braun 370 because it uses two AA cell batteries and is foolproof when it comes to keeping it off when not in use. To

turn it on you first have to completely turn the unit one hundred and eighty degrees inside its case, where the blades are otherwise protected. The shaver is available at better chain drug stores.

Liquid Laundry Soap

I fill a two ounce bottle with Woolite before I go off on a journey. It's gentle enough for all my gear, does the job when I'm on the road and rinses out of garments easier than attempting to use liquid machine soap in a sink at the campground or hotel.

Here's a little trick. Need to run your laundry at your campsite, but there are no facilities? Simply fill a dry bag full of water, squirt in some liquid laundry soap. Stuff your dirty clothes in and agitate with your hand for several minutes. Rinse, agitate some more, rinse and hang dry.

Chapter Thirteen

Before and After the Ride

If you're planning ahead there are things you'll want to take care of before and after your ride so that your final preparation goes smoothly.

Make Your List and Check it Twice

Throughout this book you'll find the essential list of the things I carry when I ride. Now it's time for you to craft up your own. Your list will never be finished, it will always be changing and evolving. Create your list in a word processing program and update it as often as you need to.

Each time you ride print out your list and when it's time to pack check off each item as you assemble your gear together.

I have a habit of not physically checking off items on my list. Inevitably that results in me forgetting to bring something on the ride. As long as I stick with the checkmark system I do pretty well.

Pack One or Two Days Beforehand

If you plan to ride on Sunday, don't wait until Sunday morning to start packing. Pack Saturday so you can take care of any last minute details and have everything ready to go the next morning.

There are a lot of things that happen in the hour just before you ride. Getting your gear on, putting your luggage on the bike, doing a pre-ride inspection of the bike to be sure tires are inflated properly, brakes work, fluids are correct and so on. Now, if you end up packing on top of all this your head will be spinning as you ride out the driveway.

If you're planning a multi-day trip, it's best to start packing at least two days ahead of time. This gives you time to get to the store and stock up on last-minute things, repair tears in your tent or raingear and replenish things you may have used up along the way.

Freshen Up

Consumables like sunscreens, eyewear cleaning fluids, shower soap and shampoo have a way of getting down to nothing. It's best to take care of refilling these before your trip rather than figuring out while you're on the road that you don't have enough shampoo to get you through the week. This is also something you may want to do early on in your riding season as well.

Chapter Fourteen

Ready for the Journey?

Every motorcycle trip is an adventure all its own. From beautiful days to hail storms and high winds, from worry-free miles to blow outs and mechanical gremlins, you never know what lies ahead.

Hopefully this book has prepared you for your journey and you're better able to deal with situations with ease than ever before.

In the Northwest where I live (also know as the "North Wet"), we're blessed with a variety of landscapes. Two exquisite mountain ranges, the Olympics and Cascades, a stunning canyon land region in the Columbia River Gorge, rolling wheat and farm lands in the Palouse, and some of the best back roads I've ever traveled, both pavement and dirt.

My trips through Washington and the Northwest just get better and better because I've gotten better at the art of packing for the motorcycle ride.

I hope you've enjoyed this book and that it makes your trip that much better for having read it.

Have a great ride!